Plum Pond

by Bud Hamilton
illustrated by Deborah Colvin Borgo

Core Decodable 30

I0806536

McGraw Hill Education

Bothell, WA • Chicago, IL • Columbus, OH • New York, NY

MHEonline.com

Send all inquiries to:
McGraw-Hill Education
8787 Orion Place
Columbus, OH 43240

ISBN: 978-0-02-145303-0
MHID: 0-02-145303-9

Printed in Canada.

9 10 11 12 KOD 24

The sun was up at Plum Pond.

"I spot black ducks," said Jill.

"Plus I spot a gull," said Gramps.

"Look on the stump," said Gramps.
"It's a slug."

A big bug sat in mud.
"Did it get stuck?" said Jill.

Plum Pond is fun!